A Million Brown Girls

A Memoir

D1572276

Lesleigh Montgomery

For information contact Authors Inside
P.O. Box 293, Oceano, CA 93475
Email: info@authorsinside.org
Website: www.authorsinside.com

Paperback ISBN: 978-1-954736-32-0
eBook ISBN: 978-1-954736-33-7

To Sam Henry King my grandfather who laid the strong foundation of faith in God in my life. My grandmother, Minnie Lee King, the quiet, strong matriarch of the family God fearing and our own Queen of the King family.

To my mother Lula Mae King Montgomery the most beautiful, strong example of what a mother should be. I miss you every day.

To my children, Aikilah & Armon Eslava, and my son, Michael King Dejerion Williams, rest in peace. I've done nothing perfect in life except birth 3 lovely children.

To Mary & James Manning the most selfless people I've ever known truly God sent, and a living example of agape love.

To all those who have supported my dreams, visions and goals over the years who have never given up on me, I say thank you! Friends and family are everything besides God.

To my Aunt Gloria and Uncle R.H. King, who have been a constant support to me throughout this time, but more important 2 people who without hesitation put their lives on pause to raise my son Michael until God called him home on 3/23/2020.

To all else, I love you…Thank you!

INTRODUCTION

A Million Brown Girls Is a collection of some of my own personal real-life struggles and triumphs while walking out of a 25-year prison sentence. When I titled this book, "A Million Brown Girls" I envisioned not only my African American sistahs but all those whose ancestors roamed not only the open land of Africa but all the way to the Islands of Jamaica. I think of every shade that represents Cambodia, Puerto Rico, Mexico all the way to the Pacific Islanders. Overall, there are too many to name, but you're all included.

I hold in my heart every brown girl in the world as she struggles with her own bouts of pain, heartache and loss. My hope is that in sharing this non-fiction testament of my life is that you will find encouragement, hope and strength in God while rediscovering the true beauty of who you are. My overall message is there is healing in your hurting, there's power that comes from pain, and there's winning in our worship! Be brave, be courageous, be beautiful brown girls no matter what you're up against.

Phil 4:13 promises, "I can do all things through Christ who strengthens me." NKJV

Throughout this book, there will be scriptures to refer to. I encourage all readers to not only read the portions highlighted but to feed on whole chapters. In doing so my prayer is that you would become familiar with the author, the text as well as the themes and purpose of each book in the Bible. God Bless...

"Be diligent to present yourself approved to God, a worker who does not need to be ashamed, rightly dividing the word of truth." 2 Timothy 2:15 NKJV

"Train up a child in the way he should go, and when he is old he will not depart from it." Prov 22:6 NKJV

To my grandfather Sam King who instilled this very scripture into my being as a young child as well as thread by thread the existence of my faith…thank you "Dad" for I've not departed from the ways of God.

Who said you can't have grown up in a loving, warm home where you not only had 3 older siblings to look after you, but also 2 parents, 2 grandparents, and most anything you wanted? Well, I did with God at the very center of it all yet i still ended up serving a 25-year sentence in Prison at the young age of 26. I was spoiled rotten; even had a t-shirt I remember I'd wear to school as proof. Memories of birthdays, holidays, weekend road trips - whatever the occasion there were always tons of family and good food that kept everyone smiling.

School was always a good place to be. I had lots of friends, played sports, never missed a field trip, or school photos. For all intents and purposes, one could conclude that I was quite popular. Thanks to my mother as well as Enice, my mother's common law husband of 20+ years and the man who raised me as his own - I missed out on absolutely nothing. Life was good for me growing up, and I especially loved spending weekends with my grandparents which is where my deep faith in God was planted in my heart, and like that of the mustard seed it has flourished into my all-sustaining living water, and well of life.

Choir practice on Saturdays, church all day Sunday, and 12 o'clock prayer in the front room until, "Dad" (my grandfather) saw fit to get off our knees on Mondays. This was what we did in the King family everyone knew it, respected it, and partook in it as we trusted in the living God Sam H. King introduced all kids to. For that I'm forever grateful. I'm sure you're asking how did I, a young lady 26 years old who came from such a loving family with elders who did all they could to instill good morals and values in me, end up doing 25 years in prison.

To every black, brown, or person of color sitting in a jail or prison cell, whether having been falsely accused or actually guilty, I come to serve notice there is still hope, love, joy and peace to be found when you decide to put your faith in Christ Jesus as Lord and savior over your life.

To answer the question, how did I end up spending a quarter century of my life in prison? Many bad choices, coupled with a decision that changed the whole trajectory of my life. Moreover, and more important, that of my children's lives as well. My eldest 2 were two months from turning 5 and 6 years old. Not to mention I was pregnant with my last child who was brutally and violently murdered 4 years, 10 months, and 12 days before my release. No matter where we come from, or what our story is or becomes, my goal in sharing my life story is to prove that no matter how dark it gets, how low you feel or alone there's always hope. He who promises to stick closer than a brother, his name is Jesus. I dare you to try Him.

This book is dedicated to all those who are presently or formerly incarcerated and found themselves surrounded by the dark shadows of despair. Yet once the light of God's love enveloped you, your eyes lifted to the hills from whence comes your help. (Ps. 121: 1-2) NKVJ

Thank God for His amazing grace, His son's saving power as well as the comforter (Holy Spirit) who is our keeper through it all. Finally, to all who are still physically locked up, DO NOT forget you have a friend in Jesus.

This is my story, one of struggles, pain, drugs, and wrong turns that led to jail, and ultimately prison. A story of faith, hope, love, restoration, and finally my release where I will begin to put the pieces of my life back together. My prayer is that through me opening up my heart while sharing pieces of my life, one if not many, will find the courage to continue living even in the face of one's darkest days and nights.

My eyes were finally opened, my head clear and I was free. The only thing was physically I wasn't free. I was in a musty, dark jail cell awaiting my fate, looking at 320 months in W.C.C.W. prison, and for those who can't compute with ease, 25 years. I was pregnant with my 3rd child, my second son, due to give birth any day with my trial being put off continually (prosecutorial strategy) in order for me not to gain sympathy from the jury. It was important that I looked like a villain, not a victim...a cold-hearted murderer, something I'm not.

I was free, free from the street life, the using and selling of drugs, but now I was really free to find what I had lost as a child. I had the right as well as the space to dream again, to believe in myself again. I had no clue what this would look like, but the God I'd always known since a very young age, well He was about to show me what a true transformation of heart and soul looked like. He had me right where he needed me, and there was nowhere to run except in His direction.

Before I get into the meat and potatoes of my story, let me just put it out there, as I write this book, I'll be 50 years old in 2 weeks and 1 day. I've been fighting tooth and nail to write this book against all signs to proceed. Now understand this, one's past doesn't define one's present. However, some of the things I'll confess as being a part of my journey has also become instrumental in propelling me into my purpose. Moreover, every last piece fits into its perfect place and has made me who I am today.

I envision speaking before thousands - in fact, God has shown me several times over. I see myself witnessing to many children in underprivileged neighborhoods, marginalized because their parents don't fit into a socioeconomic status that would allow them to dream beyond their "hood" or "ghetto". Whoever will listen, I want to be a voice that speaks for "a million brown girls" as well as boys, because Queens give birth to Kings, as well as Kings to Queens. Therefore, it is my duty to help change the direction in as many lives God allows me to touch.

Let me be very clear, I've shot at people (not confirming nor denying) shooting a person, or persons. I've robbed, held a man at gunpoint, stolen, beat people up in the streets, sold drugs, used drugs, ran with gangs and the list goes on.

I've watched a man shot to death right in front of my eyes, I've been held at gunpoint myself. However, I've never murdered anyone. I tell you this to show how God will protect and keep you. Twenty-two plus years into my 25-year sentence I thought the time was now to share my story of hope, faith, trust, etc. I know what I'm going to share isn't just my story, but a representation of a million brown girls worldwide.

Keep the faith! Shout out to my prison counselor F. Reyes.

LOSS

Yes Furthermore, I count everything as loss compared to the possession of the priceless privilege (the overwhelming preciousness, the surpassing worth and supreme advantage) of knowing Christ Jesus my Lord and of progressively becoming more deeply and intimately acquainted with Him [of perceiving and recognizing and understanding Him more fully and clearly]. For His sake I have lost everything, and I consider it all to be mere rubbish (refuse, dregs), in order that I may win (gain) Christ (the Anointed One) Philippians 3:8 AMP

Song: Even Me
Artist: Crystal Aikin

Song: When I Pray
Artist: Doe

I was in a cold, small sterile room shaken, confused, scared, and so many things going through my mind. How many hours had passed there's no way for me to accurately recall, my children had been taken from me, held secretly in the same police station unbeknownst to me, and I didn't find out until I was on my way to booking being charged with First-degree murder. My life of using and selling drugs had caught up to me in the worst way, and more important than me losing my freedom, I'd lost my children as well.

On a cold December night, my life changed, and although in the midst of it all, it looked like it was all for the worse. However, 20+ years in and I can without a doubt tell you my mind, body, and soul have never felt freer. I've witnessed countless women lose their children to the state, some even died due to their mother's addiction, or lifestyle. Looking back, in hindsight knowing everything I've been through, and admittedly everything I put my children through, God has truly been faithful.

My two oldest children went to my mother upon my incarceration, and my unborn son went to live with my uncle and auntie who raised him as if he were their own. Over the course of my sentence, I was never without having my children in my life apart from 4.5 years my two eldest were kept from my mother, a very long story, and yet still didn't stop me from knowing how truly blessed I was.

I remember telling the Judge, "It's all a big loss, nobody won." When I was sentenced to a 25-year bid to be confined in/at Washington Correction Center for Women (WCCW), I saw no light, felt no joy, and had no hope for a future. I was 26 years old, leaving behind 2 children, ages 4 and 5 years old, with one of whom I'd just given birth to. Moreover, I was on my way to spend almost half my life in prison by the time I was due to be released. Unbeknownst to me, I was actually getting ready to walk through the doors that would allow me to regain all I'd lost, and more, living the life or what I'd thought was "the life."

From the age of 15-25, I experienced some things most people only hear about; violence, homelessness, and being kidnapped by a man whom I trusted only because he was close to a family member of mine. I've been raped, molested, mentally as well as emotionally abused, just to name a few. Yet, walking out this 25-year sentence physically alone falling asleep night after night looking at these cold barren walls waiting to suck the life out of me has at times been unbearable.

However, on the other side of the coin, it's been absolutely liberating to know true freedom again, the freedom one feels before one's innocence is stolen.

As I sit pondering on friends, family, as well as my youngest child…yeah, I'll get into how he and I will never get to do any of the things he longed for upon my release, or what my heart so desired to be with all 3 of my children outside of prison wires. He was violently murdered at the age of 19, almost 2 months to the day he would have turned 20 years old. Rest your soul in peace M.K.D.W. 5/24/00-3/23/2020.

As human beings temporarily residing here on earth, none of us are exempt; we will all suffer loss(es) of many kinds. Whether losing a job, best friend, spouse/loved one, and at times even a child. Loss visits us all. I say old age, if we're lucky would be a gift, but no matter how you look at it, loss is painful and at times paralyzing. Loss, if one isn't careful, can lead to irreversible mental instabilities due to depression (depressed state of mind).

When I was sentenced to 25 years, my first thought as well as my fear was, 'I'm gonna get out to no mother and no grandmother,' but I never thought I'd lose a child. Thinking back almost 6 years now, losing my mother was the hardest loss I've suffered. In fact, it was the most difficult time hands down I've endured.

Thinking back on it (the day I was told the horrible news) or shall I say the news I had already known, because around midnight, on 10/26/16 as I sat on my bunk praying, *"Not my will but yours be done, Lord,"* it was then I felt my mother transition into eternity. Early that morning when my counselor called me into his office, my sister, Natalie, spoke the words, "Your mom passed away." I was on the phone with her because my brother was in no shape to talk at all, it took everything in me to stay seated even writing this, it's all hard to recall. That's how completely devastated I was.

There are no words that can convey the heaviness of grief that lay upon me. I literally felt I would die of a broken heart. One of my deepest prayers was to be able to have more time with my mother again, to be able to give back to her in some way for all the years of love and sacrifice she'd given to her family as well as her children. It may come as a shock, as well as a surprise to most, when I've also lost my youngest child (son), but my mother's passing hit me the hardest. It hurt me while sending waves of pain so deep in my soul that I didn't think I'd ever come out of that dark place of depression; I saw no way of escape. The Bible tells believers in the book of I Cor. 10:13, "No temptation has overtaken you except such as is common to man; but God…able to bear it."

Depression has the power to overwhelm anyone as well as every demonic spirit that is not like God. Yet, He that promised is faithful to keep you. I'm here, I'm well in body, mind, and spirit praise God. I've asked myself why my mother's death was the hardest to get through. Losing my grandmother 4 years prior was tough, but as with my mother, God gave me time to process as well as to prepare. My granny (Mom) as we all called her, she lived to almost 90, so for most, they would call that a "good life."

I guess one could say with a sentence as lengthy as mine in the back of my mind sad as it is to say, I just didn't expect my Granny to see me walk out of prison. However, I did hold onto every hope as well as believed my mother would be there. Even now, thinking back I have no answers to why it was the hardest death to get through and Lord knows there's still no getting over it. As a friend of mine (Vonnie) yells from outside my window, "You look sad, what are you writing?" Obviously, the pain still showing on my face because I'm reliving that awful day. October 26th was the day she was born, and the day she went home to be with the Lord.

I'd like to be clear, the bond shared between my baby, Michael, and I was like that of no other, we were very close, and he was with me every single day at the beginning of my incarceration. When all I saw was darkness and despair all I had was a King to sing to while enjoying him dancing in my womb. He was a precious gift from the very beginning, which is why I named him King, and as he lived his light shone brightly. He was loved by everyone who came in contact with him. I miss his presence, his giggle, his eyes that mirrored my own as well as his voice that held a deepness of the man he was becoming.

As a king kicked inside my womb, never did I imagine we'd be separated so soon. Time wasn't on our side, but we chose to ride; the hills, valleys, and curves of my incarceration added pressure to our separation.

> Queen I am, Queen I be, can't take
> away my king from me… R.I.P., Son.

I wrote this in honor of my son, "King" after his death. Life will never be the same, you'll never be forgotten.

I've heard all my life a mother shouldn't bury her child, but I'm here to tell you no matter the order the pain is no less. I'm a living witness to God's promise made in 2 Cor. 12:9 (Amp) in my fleshly weakness God's grace was and always has been sufficient.

"But He said to me, My grace (My favor and loving-kindness and mercy) is enough for you [sufficient against any danger and enables you to bear the trouble manfully]; for My strength and power are made perfect (fulfilled and completed) and show themselves most effective in [your] weakness. Therefore, I will all the more gladly glory in my weaknesses and infirmities, that the strength and power of Christ (the Messiah) may rest (yes, may pitch a tent over and dwell) upon me!

There is nothing like the covering of God being under the shadow of the Almighty as He shields you from life's storms. I'm only here right now giving a written testimony of pieces of my life story, because of the grace of God, the way He carried me through my son's death still amazes me. I'm reminded of a conversation I had with a couple of close friends who stood by watching me go through yet another devastating loss.

I said, "It's like a slap in the face when you claim you're praying for me, but when you see your prayers manifested before your eyes, your response is, "Oh friend you're in shock." It's so funny how we believers pray for peace, supernatural healing, grace under fire as well as favor, yet when we see it we don't believe it.

The word of God says, His word will go out, and not return void (Is. 55:11) Amp. "So shall my word be that goes forth out of my mouth: it shall not return to me void [without producing any effect, useless], but it shall accomplish that which I please and purpose, and it shall prosper in the thing for which I sent it." With that being said, to any Bible-believing woman of faith in the one true living God, DO NOT pray for something to then turn around when you see God move to discredit His power; He is the Great I Am.

Processing the loss of a loved one will never be an easy feat, and when it's your child it's even harder. I was faced with the task of processing while grieving simultaneously in a very unnatural and exposed way due to being in prison. I wasn't afforded the same luxuries I was when my grandmother and mother passed (attending both their funerals by escort). No, I wasn't even 1 of 10 people (immediate family) who would see him committed back to the earth.

Michael was killed at the peak of COVID-19, which had hit the world like a sledgehammer on wood, shattering everyone's ability to think, comprehend, or understand what was happening. Moreover, in hindsight what would happen to our living a "normal life" or lives after the dust settled? Nobody knew, and I was left with 4 pictures of my boy in a box, that was my goodbye. The loss I'm still trying to come to terms with, and in all honesty, it seems quite unreal. However, what is real is God's amazing grace as well as His strength. Ps. 73:26 amp "My flesh and my heart may fail, but God is the rock and firm strength of my heart and my portion forever." I call on Him daily for all my needs and I encourage my readers to do the same.

I'd like to speak to all women of color who have been a victim of abuse of any kind, to women who have put themselves in compromising positions to survive or otherwise. Suffering great loss doesn't have to be losing a loved one, loss comes in all forms especially being a woman. I've lost my respect, integrity, my good name, and more, which now forces me to wear a title that is a completely inaccurate description of who I am. In fact, I am a child of a King, as well as all who have accepted

Jesus as Lord over their life. The Bible says, in the book of Revelation 19:16 amp, "And on His garment (robe) and on His thigh He has a name (title) inscribed, King of Kings and Lord of Lords." Jesus has paid in full, and our past is under the blood, "His" blood. All things have been made new. Your name, your character, integrity, etc.

I charge you to walk in your newness, not in the ways of old. It's taken me over 20 years to show up as the woman I am today. However, make no mistake, I'm far from complete, finished, or done. I'm constantly being placed back on the potter's wheel, back into the fiery furnace, and until God's plan(s) or purpose is fulfilled in our lives, He will send us around the mountain again and again and again. This is called a work in progress!

Usually, when a person finds themselves in jail or prison it's safe to deduce that one was living a life that put one's character into question. Similarly, trust and dependability along with a lot of other great qualities a person who is living an upright life possesses, goes right down the drain. Furthermore, it's almost impossible to redeem oneself, but I'm here to tell you with hard work and determination anything is possible.

What I've learned over time is true transformation takes time, effort, and mindfulness it's a process similar to that of a butterfly becoming itself. The caterpillar is a butterfly, and the butterfly is a caterpillar yet in order for us to emerge beautiful as we once were we have to come full circle. Transformation is being honest with who you are, what you've done, and most important of all, where you want to go from here. Are you willing to put in the work? Willing to strip down to complete vulnerability? To come face to face with every demon that has held you captive? That's where true transformation begins.

If you said yes to all 3 of those questions - if you have accepted Jesus as Lord over your life, then trust Him with the rest. Ask Him to make all things new in your life, and heart as He cleanses you daily from shame, guilt, unforgiveness, etc. Thank Him as the weight of it all falls off of you. I believe in the precious name of Jesus You're New! Amen.

"In the beginning was the Word, and the Word was with God, and the Word was God. [2]He was in the beginning with God. [3]All things were made through Him, and without Him nothing was made that was made. [4]In Him was life, and the life was the light of men. [5]And the light shines in the darkness, and the darkness did not comprehend it." John 1:1-5 (NKJV)

It's in the quiet times alone in the dark when the walls of despair are squeezing me tight whispering, "There is no light at the end of the tunnel" However, there is no light if darkness doesn't exist. Therefore, one has to plunge into the darkness of life to be bathed in the light/love of Jesus where our hope is then found.

My prayer is that in sharing what is definitely a few of the hardest things I've lost thus far in my life, you can find hope, courage, and strength to continue on with the help of the Lord Jesus as well as the Holy Spirit and all His benefits.

OPEN HEART

"A man who has friends must himself be friendly, But there is a friend who sticks closer than a brother." Prov. 18:24

Song: You Amaze Me
Artist: Vicki Yohe

In Merriam-Webster's Dictionary, the word friend is defined as 1) One attached to another by respect, or affection. 2) Acquaintance. In the last 23 years, I have experienced many relationships. I have befriended a good number of women as well as become a friend. However, it is very important not to get an acquaintance confused with a friend. I urge you to know the difference.

I began meeting lots of different women especially since I was very pregnant when I was arrested. Open heart...in hindsight looking back God had opened the window in order for many to see, not my charges, not my growing belly, but my heart. As I slowly began opening up and talking to those around me, I began seeing hearts, bleeding hearts, hearts broken which caused me to do what we as humans are made in the image of God to do; show compassion and love.

I had no clue about all the lives God would empower me to touch, no clue of the lifelong friends I'd make, or long relationships that would end in silence existing no more. There is a quote by Bishop T.D. Jakes I read in his 365-day W.T.A.L. journal, he asserts, "One must feed that which you want to live and starve what you wish to die in your life." Clearly, this was metaphorically written, and what I'm sure was implied to our spiritual life. Yet, what is our spiritual life if not manifested in the physical?

I'm reminded of another saying that is supported by the Word of God, Ecclesiastes 3:1 AMP "TO EVERYTHING there is a season, and a time for every matter or purpose under heaven." With that being said, everything and everyone has a purpose, a season, or a reason in our lives. Although I've met countless wonderful, amazing people over the years there are but a few I call friends. Thank you to each one of you my heart remains open to your love as well as your friendship.

I'd been sitting around on February 7, 2022, when I decided to call my friend as I often do when I have important issues or news to share. I wanted to share with Mary that I'd decided the time was now to begin writing my book; In all her excitement at the end of our conversation, she told me after a brief pause… "Lesleigh, write with an open heart."

I never knew, or shall I say, I've never experienced an open heart, unconditional love as well as so many beautiful gifts wrapped up in one person until I met Mary Manning. Our story, and our friendship, began in the year 2000. A few months after I was arrested, I was sent to the downtown County Jail where Mary was a Chaplain. She was a volunteer who did Chapel services as well as 1-on-1 visits with people. According to Mary, she recalls someone at the Jail told her I could use some encouragement. Shortly after that, we began meeting, and mind you there were many days I wouldn't even come out to our visit. However, Mary remained faithful, always checking in one visit after the next.

Thinking back, I remember a day that has since become a flashbulb memory. Mary and I both still tear up whenever we speak of this day, I even now writing get misty-eyed. Honestly, there weren't many visits I wasn't crying. This day was no different as we looked into one another's eyes, she spoke, "I'm going to do this time with you Lesleigh, no matter if it's all of it, or part of it, I'm here with you." ...twenty-three years later as I'm writing this book, she's still here loving me unconditionally, supporting me, and not just her, but her amazing husband Jim who I've grown very close to as well. Both of them have been hands down the epitome of an open heart, love, and friendship.

My friendship with Mary over the years showed me what real patience, understanding, and grace looked like in human form. Having a friend who truly believed in me when I myself didn't believe in me. Her showing me love, and support as well as a genuine open-heart friendship, has kept me strong as I strive to be a good friend to others.

God's transformation work in me has brought me heart-to-heart with some wonderful women, and as I write with my heart open, as transparent as I'm able to be, my hope is I'll be received with love, grace, and an open heart. Over 2 decades our friendship has grown deep, wide, and stronger than ever. We've shared some of the most intimate details of our lives. There have been painful racial inequalities (mine included), witnessing many defeats over and over.

Over 23 years, thus far, there have been countless, devastating heart-breaking losses and defeats through the judicial system, the most recent in 2020.

June 5th
Attention: Carla Lee/Dan Satterburg

As I sit looking out the window of my room a little over 1 week removed from spending 30 days in segregation/isolation due to Covid-19, yes another outbreak! It was then 10 months

*after the fact I had realized the time has come
to write this letter. I can't begin to put into
words all the pain, confusion, anger and the
disgust I felt that not only myself but my family,
friends and loved ones suffered by the
mishandling of my case from the KCPAO. I want
to also mention I think it was less than
professional as well as ethical to have led me to
believe I was supported 110% yet I was
dropped. No my lawyer was left to deliver the
devastating, disappointing and disheartening
news, "They're unable to move forward with
your resentencing." Still in disbelief I'm left
shaking my head. Again, almost a year later I
needed my voice to be heard, and to represent
every brown girl/woman who has been the
recipient of a miscarriage of justice (your words,
not mines), by way of an unjust justice system.*

*As we know there are many, but I write to a
woman first then to a woman who looks like me;
a woman I'm sure has been handed many
disappointments, in addition to hearing the ring
of NO time and time again. What's most difficult
for me to understand Carla if I may address you
by your first name is the politics of it all. The
Wins v. Losses in an already sick "justice"
system was the most important voice to be
heard, and looking back on it all I can still hear
you, "we're posturing to win!" Funny thing is if,
the KCPAO would have let the Judge do his job
who's to say we wouldn't have won? I'm not at
all upset at the fact my victims don't want to see
me released, I am however upset that the
KCPAO who so passionately asserted over and
over how much they supported my resentencing as well as my release would deny
Judge Oisho the opportunity to do his
job...make the final decision as to whether he
saw fit to affirm the motion between your office
and my lawyer.*

*I'd also like to ask that the lifetime NCO be
fluid seeing as I've been on the receiving end*

from (2) people in the family I'm to have no contact with. I know your office has been made aware. Carla I'm sure your days are busy with files, cases, as well as DOC#s which is why I will bring this to a close. However, before I close I will say this. Everything we do in life effects someone else. I have made many mistakes, caused hurt to many people as well as mislead, whether with intent or not. In doing so I've learned in the process to ask for forgiveness, and how important it is to extend it while growing through it all.

I'm a woman who is still licking her wounds. However, I'm a strong courageous woman by way of experience and pain. I chose to move forward with the knowledge that no matter how much darkness in ones life the light will break forth again. There's a quote I love by the great Maya Angelou, she states, "You may encounter many defeats, but you must not be defeated. In fact, it may be necessary to encounter the defeats, so you can know who you are, what you can rise from, how you can still come out of it." However small or insignificant my experience was to the KCPAO I need you to know it's taken a toll on me, my friends and family. It's been extremely hard on all involved even to this day, and you played a HUGE role in the crushing!

In the grand scheme of things I know my true hope is in God. I'm still in search of the door, or doors that will unlock a complete peace in me concerning the whole ordeal that laid on me like a heavy weight, still does some days. In fact, it could be perhaps in writing this letter I will feel a sense of peace as well as closure. I do know I'm closing the door and this chapter which feels alot different than having the door SHUT in my face with absolutely no regard as to how it effected as well as affected me.

I'm moving forward with courage while reminding myself that life is like that of a mighty, fast moving, rushing body of water *taking with it by force some things while it allows others to rest in it's vastness. I'm thankful for what I have left. My faith, my dignity, my character, my integrity, but most of all an openness of heart.*

Sincerely,

Ms. L. Montgomery

Through it all, Mary and I have had our times of happiness, and joy, along with many celebrations, as I've accomplished much during my time of incarceration. Not only my academic accomplishments, but moral, spiritual, and mental, all of which have been instrumental in me being the woman I am today.

I'm as close to whole as I felt as a child, a very young 5-year-old little girl when memories were that of joy, smiles, and laughter, and before my innocence was stolen. Figuratively speaking, I'm now a butterfly seconds away from bursting forth from my cocoon, 24 months from release into the next stage of my life.

As I've grown, matured, struggled through navigating the breaking down and rebuilding myself to being happy, proud of as well as content with the woman I've become when I look in the mirror, there's been a woman standing by my side changing hats along the way. Mary has been a role model, spiritual advisor, confidant and so much more - modeling for me a 26-year-old black girl from the "hood" (low socioeconomic status) what true love of a friend looks like.

I've had the luxury, space, and time to uncover my capabilities, earning college degrees, learning to transcribe braille, and becoming a certified professional pet groomer through a very credible agency. (IPG). Time alone allows one to get better acquainted with oneself, knowing what you will and will not accept as well as making informed decisions about what you want in life. However, you have to be ready and willing to step into a space that will breed new life. As you shed layers, and every variation of color that camouflage has to hide or disguise the real you. It's in that space you'll uncover one beautiful color after the next, and then sooner than later the butterfly comes forth...a brand new you.

"Therefore, if anyone is in Christ, he is a new creation; old things have passed away; behold, all things have become **new**." 2 Cor. 5:17 NKJV

God's bonds are not easily broken. Similarly, friendships open to forgiveness, and grace as well as two individuals reaching out for one another - that's the making of a lasting friendship.

"In Him was life, and the life was the light of men. And the light shines in the darkness, and the darkness did not comprehend it." John 1:4-5 NKJV

As women and men of God, we are sojourners here on earth merely passing through. Moreover, as light-bearing vessels, it's our responsibility to be alert in the spirit. Only by, and through, diligent prayer can our spiritual eyes and ears remain acute because it's not only as the word of God says in Proverbs 27:17 (NKJV), "As iron sharpens iron, So a man sharpens the countenance of his friend." Being aware in the Spirit is key, along with staying fully armored in order to recognize the enemy's trickery. Stay watchful, praying at all times.

It's important to remember that darkness, deceit, and every other trick of the enemy comes in many forms as I mentioned in the last chapter, depression being one of many. Seek. Seek. Seek the light of the Lord that you may find fullness of joy. I've shared many friendships in my life, each individually playing their part at different stages in my life. However, as I've found to be very true, some more than others will hold a very dear place in your heart. I'm not quite sure what Mary felt about where she was in life when God brought us to an intersecting point, but what I do know is then as well as now, she is the light and love of Christ in my life.

Let me be clear, on my journey, there have been many members from One Body of Christ who have been instrumental in my growth spiritually, emotionally, educationally, and more. Moreover, I take little credit for the woman I've become. I've only followed as close to obedient while God led me through hills, and valleys. He even carried me in the palm of his hand when I fell from the highest cliffs. The Lord has a way of giving you what you need, not what you want at times. He will tuck you nice and snug in the cleft while you rest. He will cover you like a warm blanket with those specific to your needs at a particular time. I say thank you to all who were closest to me through my toughest times.

God's bonds are sometimes stronger and run deeper than the blood that is shared between relatives. I won't name every one of you that most definitely holds room in my heart, just know I write with you in mind.

"For all who are led by the Spirit of God are sons of God. For [the Spirit which] you have now received [is] not a spirit of slavery to put you once more in bondage to fear, but you have received the Spirit of adoption [the Spirit producing sonship] in [the bliss of] which we cry, Abba (Father)! Father! The Spirit Himself [thus] testifies together with our own spirit, [assuring us] that we are children of God…" Romans 8:14-18 (AMP)

I am truly a blessed woman, and my life is richer with all my extended family.

FAITH

But without faith it is impossible to please and be satisfactory to Him. For whoever would come near to God must [necessarily] believe that God exists and that He is the rewarder of those who earnestly and diligently seek Him [out]. Hebrews 11:6 (AMP)

Now faith is the substance of things hoped for, the evidence of things not seen. Hebrews 11:1 (NKJV)

Song: "I'll trust you Lord", "I call you Faithful"
Artist: Donnie McClurkin

Hoping, in addition to trusting in God in the face of whatever comes your way, believing in God Almighty who is unseen yet alive and ever-present. In the beginning, I didn't have a clue how strong my faith would become, or how it would be tested, but looking back over the last two decades I can without a doubt say I'm grateful for the trials, the many hills I've had to climb, as well as my Valley experiences. Over this chapter, I will open the window giving you an unobstructed view into some of the most difficult times I've had to endure. Moreover, times I've had to completely trust God through it all.

As the Bible clearly states in Hebrews 11:6, one has to believe in the god that you come to, and if I didn't know anything at all I knew God was real, alive, and true in my life. At times, like most children, whether we're looking at things in a natural/earthly sense, or spiritual, we as kids (as we so often do) walk in disobedience. However, like loving parents, God is always there to clean us up and love us back to a place of wholeness.

I'm thankful today that as I reached out to the only one thing in my life that never failed me, He - God grabbed hold of me with such tenderness while leading me on a journey that has proved as the word of God states in chapter 8 of The Book of Romans 28th verse "And we know all things work together for good to those who love god, to those who are called according to his purpose." (NKJV). I can truly say I'm a better human being, friend, mother, sister, etc. he has worked everything the enemy meant for evil in my life God has turned it around for good. Faith is a hard pill to swallow as my grandmother would say, especially when one's life is in the hands of another. However, if I'm going to trust one with my life God is the best (trustee).

In 1999 I was arrested. In early 2000, one evening while attending a chapel service at KCJ, one of the volunteers who had taken the opportunity to pray before the service ended asked me if she could pray for me. I was 8.5 months pregnant at the time, and I took a breath, very reluctant for some reason. I can't say before this that I've ever had someone prophesy over me. Well, as she prayed, she began telling me that I wouldn't do it all the time (I was sentenced to 25 years). However, 23 years later, I am moved to write this book. Why? Because God said so.

For those who aren't aware of what it means to have a man or woman prophesy over you, it's when a Believer is used by God to utter divine

28

inspiration and encourage or exhort. One of the nine gifts of the Holy Spirit (see I Cor. 12). I have held on to this promise for over two decades while exhausting every level of appeal trying to find relief. In late 2018, or early 2019, I was given what I had imagined was my last chance. God was about to do it. I was weak, exhausted, tired, and angry at times over 20 years into a 25-year sentence. However, the battle wasn't over, I've been accepted as a candidate for resentencing - 2020 was to be my year!

To go home 5 years early was music to my ears, and God was faithful to his promise. March 23rd, 2020, things had been moving forward. I was set to get a court date and be released no later than 90 days after everything with my sentence was changed in/through records. Ready to share finally from beginning to end my testimony when things took a sudden turn. Before I share the devastating sudden turn, let me ask you a question, when all is well do you stay in a space spiritually trusting God when he pivots? Honestly speaking, I can't say I've always been there. However, through prayer, and hindsight vision you'll come to realize, like I have, that God will lovingly get you through, even when He pivots.

On March 23rd, I woke up, and like most days' things felt and fell in place in a normal type of way. It wasn't long after COVID-19 had hit but I'll get into that later, I went to my appointment outside of my living unit to pick up new clothes. As I returned to my unit - no sooner than I'd walked in, I heard my name called on the loudspeaker (not always a good sign). It was then I heard someone yell, "There she is!" Before I knew it, I was being ushered into the unit supervisor's office at which time my heart sank, because I knew from the look on his face something was terribly wrong. As he instructed me to have a seat he said in a very serious voice, "You need to call home." OMG! This is bad. However, there was nothing that could have prepared me for what I heard on the other end of the phone line.

My oldest brother in a very shaken, quiet nearly inaudible voice said, "Mikey is dead, he was murdered last night." He along with his cousin who passed away the next day. All I remember was screaming, "No!" Even now writing this book, over 2 years later, I'm still drawing a blank. Two family members, two funerals, or the lack thereof due to COVID-19 but for me, it would be the beginning of yet another death. Moreover, my baby…19 years young; he's gone.

How does one remain faith-filled as well as faithful when less than a week prior Michael and I went back and forth about who wanted my release more him or myself? In my pain, hurt, confusion, and anger I had to accept the reality of the situation; my son wouldn't be among those who love me, who have been doing this time with me. No, he'd been murdered while waiting for my release.

In life, no matter where you are you're always given a choice. I chose to trust God, to continue believing in God, but most importantly to have Faith in His presence, in His promises as well as His purpose in/through it all. I'm not saying at all it was or is even now easy because it's not! what I am saying is God's grace is all-sufficient, and He has been carrying me every day while empowering me to write, speak, and live.

I lost my grandmother in 2012. my mother in 2016, and my child in 2020. Romans 8:28 has been a for sure go to scripture because it reminds me to hold on while trusting that all will work out for my good. Again, it's not easy, but the Lord never promised this Faith walk would be easy. In fact, He said it best in John 16:33 (NKJV), "These things I have spoken to you, that in Me you may have peace. In the world you will have tribulation; but be of good cheer, I have overcome the world." In short, I want to remind us, Women and Men of faith, that tribulation(s) is anything distressing, suffering due to oppression, trying experiences, etc. However, our job is to praise, thank, and worship God in the process for as His word says, He'll never leave nor forsake us.

Losing my mother just about took me to a place mentally I couldn't come back from, so I knew I had to let go and let God! 2 Cor. 12:9 Manifested right before my eyes; His strength was made perfect in my weakness. He will carry you if you allow him. Even to this very day, my breath catches and my chest swells thinking of both my mother as well as my son...I'm left speechless. But God is still good, He's still on the throne, so no matter the promise no matter the pain just keep the Faith.

Women and men of Faith this is a call to action. As difficult as it is, and as hard as it can be in the midst of a trial or as we endure various tribulations, we have to stop putting our trust in man but rather in God who we should entrust our lives. I don't have all the answers, not even close, I don't know what good in its full and complete form will come of the various trials. However, what I do know is in the book of Ephesians 3:20 (AMP), "Now to Him Who, by (in consequence of) the [action of His] power that is at work within us, is able to [carry out His purpose and] do superabundantly, far over and above all that we [dare] ask or think [infinitely beyond our highest prayers, desires, thoughts, hopes, or dreams]–" God knows our deepest desires our visions and hope so if and when we are blindsided by life's happenings I dare you to trust him.

I never was resentenced, and after taking my family, and friends as well as myself through more than 2 years of reliving the details of my past, all I was left with was, "Lesleigh the prosecuting attorney's office will not be moving forward with your resentencing." I was devastated! Oh, that's not it, I found out six months later that I'd have to do every day of my sentence behind the razor. no work release, no graduated re-entry, nothing was available to me to go home before December 11, 2024.

The unchanging love of God is what was available to me coupled with my faith, trust, hope, and belief that all would be well. The last 20-plus years I've told my story in pieces to countless women as well as men, and I've witnessed to even more. I've made plenty of mistakes in my life while resisting along the way, but over the time of my incarceration, the best thing I've done has been to surrender to the transforming power of God. I'm still a work in progress, so even when one fails (me included), remember the promise Psalm 73:26 "My flesh and my heart may fail, but God is the Rock and firm Strength of my heart and my Portion forever."

Jesus has the ability to transcend margins, ethnicities, and socioeconomic statuses, but it's a fact that women and men of color are sentenced to excessive amounts of time in comparison to their counterparts. Your story may, or may not, mirror my story. However, what I want to witness is no matter what your particular set of circumstances may be that led you to jail, or prison, there are no walls and no razor that can hold the hope of a child of God! Be ambassadors for Christ, witness where you stand.

I've questioned many times over the past two decades, "Is my faith not strong enough?" "Am I not truly standing on the promises of God?" Believing that His word works. There have been many times in my life, since knowing Christ, as an adult while trusting in the evidence of the Holy Ghost that I've still thought, "I'm not worthy", "I lack faith", or I'm doing something wrong...the list goes on. However, I've come to trust the word of God as the gospel. Believing in what John 10:10 says, it's none other than the father of Lies with his trickery, "the enemy comes only "to steal and kill and destroy." Jesus comes to give us life and life abundantly.

The best part of that passage is the promise of abundant life. It's so imperative to our spiritual health that we are diligently exercising our faith muscles. Daily reading, prayer/meditation time focused on the Living Word of God, remember God says he's a rewarder of those who seek Him. Make it your business as I do mine to equip yourself no matter the cost, it may mean sacrificing time with friends, and loved ones, maybe even being alone for hours on end, but the reward is great. There's no better place to be than in the presence of the Holy Spirit, soaking up every ounce of the glory of God. Ask Him to open your spiritual ears, eyes, and heart to receive all He has for you while feasting on the Living Word of God.

I love to come away full when the eyes of my understanding have been opened, and when my mind is in a place to have Godly wisdom poured in. The word tells us in Mark 12:30 "And you shall love the Lord your God with all your heart, with all your soul, with all your mind, and with all your strength. This is the first commandment." When I think of this passage, I think of how I feel when I've loved A lover or friend - I'm all in, my heart is weak with love, mind, body, and soul. Everything that makes me who I am in personality, character, every little piece of me I want my lover to know. I want to share my every thought, all that makes me laugh, cry, sad, hopeful you name it, and I put all my strength into the relationship in order to see it become lasting and strong. this is how we are to love God.

There are three V's to living a life of faith; vow, vocalize, and visualize. Vow to love God, vocalize your confession in Christ as Lord, and visualize living a victorious life. SEE YOURSELF DOING, BEING, AND LIVING YOUR ABUNDANT LIFE. The word tells us in Romans 4:17, "I...and calls those things which do not exist as though they did." I'm here to tell you God's timing is not always our timing, in fact, usually, it's not but that doesn't mean to lose heart or faith in the all-powerful loving God we serve. I challenge you to take a moment to think back to a time in your life when a particular situation didn't go your way, yet when it was all said and done can you say something good still came of it?

It takes real Faith to know, or believe you'll come out on the other side of the darkest place you've experienced in life. It takes Faith to know that as you serve a spirit God that is unseen will without a doubt work all things out for your good. It's Experiencing God in his fullness that causes you to trust in his every promise. Haven't you ever held a cold cup filled with water on a hot summer day? If you have, which I imagine one has, it helps. Moreover, there's nothing like the experience of drinking a cold drink in the way it quenches that thirst. this is where full and total abandonment to trusting in Jesus comes from when you experience His faithfulness, His power, and glory. When you experience Him lovingly working life out for your good there's nothing like it.

There is a promise for every problem, and a purpose and nobody is without trouble just as we are all afforded blessings in life. However, to everything there are checks and balances, there is no good without bad, or not so good. Our test in this Faith walk is to continue moving forward pressing towards the mark. Yes, even when it's dark. even when you're sad, lonely, jobless, etc. you hold on to the Victorious One Jehovah Nissi our banner... Jesus. Thinking of the day I walk out of prison at 52 years of age - having had all of my 20s, 30s, and 40s spent in prison - I can't say it's easy to hold onto faith.

Moreover, faith that I'll be able to leave a legacy that will cause my children's and grandchildren's hearts to swell with pride, not cause their heads to drop due to the fact I've left nothing apart from memories of visits, phone calls, and letters from prison. This is the faith I've been exercising for over two decades as I've grown into the woman I am today. It took thousands of dark, lonely nights falling asleep to the same four concrete walls, it took me looking at myself in the mirror until I loved who looked back at me. It took work, and as a friend shared with me, plenty of D.A.W.G. days.

There are over a million brown girls around the world just like me holding onto hope, on to faith, as they spend countless days alone with God. I encourage you to continue believing that better days are on the way, and if you're reading this book, hold onto your faith even if it is the size of a mustard seed (Matt. 17:20 NKJV), Wherever your faith is, ask God to increase it while moving through each day believing He will.

In conclusion to this chapter on faith let me assure you I could give you so much more, but I'd like to point you to a particular portion of scripture, one that has given me hope and peace while filling me with joy. In Jeremiah 29:11-13 (AMP), God promises us a future good not evil as well as hope, but there's a second piece...we have to seek Him. Seek Him with our whole heart. Whether you found yourself in a jail cell, shelter, homeless, or in prison due to being addicted to drugs or behaviors I'm telling you I've been there. I'm a witness, a living testimony that God's goodness, His mercy, His grace, His hands are not too short that they can't pull you up and out of any situation. Hold on, my family members, to Christ Jesus, and keep the faith.

OBEDIENCE

Your word is a lamp to my feet And a light to my path. Psalms 119:105 (NKJV)

Children, obey your parents in all things, for this is well pleasing to the Lord. Colossians 3:20 (NKJV)

Proverbs 6:23 (AMP)
For the commandment is a lamp, and the whole teaching [of the law] is light, and reproofs of discipline are the way of life, [Ps. 19:8; 119:105.]

Then He said, "Take now your son, your only son Isaac, whom you love, and go to the land of Moriah, and offer him there as a burnt offering on one of the mountains of which I shall tell you." Genesis 22:2 (NKJV)

Song: Because of Who You Are.
Artist: Vicki Yohe

As I sit pondering on the word, obedience/obey, I'm wondering why there is more times than not a negative connotation attached to the word. To obey or be obedient is to submit to or follow the commands as well as the guidance of one's authority. There's an acronym for the word Bible, I have no clue who made it up, or when it surfaced. However, it makes perfect sense knowing that it's the Living Word of God. **B**asic **I**nstructions **B**efore **L**eaving **E**arth, ironic right? Our heavenly Father has made sure that we as Believers have a written Manual of his every command, and it's our job to follow in obedience While submitting to his authority, those commandments.

Trusting one's Earthly parents is just as important if not equally as important as trusting our heavenly father, and as it is written this is well pleasing to the lord. Moreover, ultimately it is God who we should aim to please at all times, and in every situation/circumstance. As we move through this chapter together, I will challenge you to look back on past experiences, missed opportunities, failed relationships, etc. whenever the spirit of God calls on you to move, but you sit still or offer forgiveness yet your pride hardens your heart while locking your lips shut.

there have been countless times when I've allowed my flesh to win over my spirit which equips me with a variety of fruit to ensure that I walk victoriously in obedience to God. Now as a child of course we ask questions like, "Why not," we tested our parents to see just how far we could go, and in the end either we listened and obeyed, or suffered the consequences of being disobedient.

Not only was I a very spoiled child, but I could also come across as hard-headed, and the older I got the more I thought I knew. In 1st Corinthians 13:11, the Bible speaks to what one should put on like clothes as one grows and becomes an adult woman or man. The question I will ask over and over is whether the fruit of the spirit of God within you is right for the picking. Let me be clear the fiery trials of one's life are what produce the ripe fruit, yes, the experiences, the pain, as well as the struggles (the fire) we all need the fire to burn out of us anything that is not like God.

It takes a lifetime so don't think for a moment this happens overnight. In fact, the word of God says in Philippians 1:6 AMP, "And I am convinced and sure of this very thing, that He who began a good work in you will continue until the day of Jesus Christ [right up to the time of his return], developing [that good work] and perfecting and bringing it to full completion in you."

Obedience takes time, effort, and patience at both ends. The teacher as well as the student, God is not only our Master, but He is also our teacher, guide, strength, counselor, and advocate. He is the great I AM. Moreover, we can do as well as become our best selves in Christ Jesus if we allow Him to lead us. I have trained dogs for service work for over 10 years, and to my surprise, I was amazed at the skills I was able to train the animals who had been rescued from shelters or the streets. I even worked with one from Hurricane Katrina. Similarly, we too have been rescued (redeemed) by the blood of Jesus back to a place of right standing with God our heavenly father who has patiently been waiting that not one should perish. Through the power of the Holy Spirit, we become obedient, and in our lives good fruit shows up through our actions, words, and deeds.

The fire produces the fruit. Fire can be used to purify, and fruit to feed. In the Garden of Eden that's all Adam and Eve had, yet they had it in abundance until disobedience led them to the great fall. Then came the fire (metaphorically speaking), all the woes of the world that mankind now would have to deal with due to one man. According to

Webster's Dictionary, the word fire has many synonyms to define or relate the word to. While I won't list them all I would like to point out a few keywords. Before I do, let me point out that also by one man was mankind given access to life, and life more abundant. Now fire is defined as such: to give life to, or spirit; to stir or enliven as well as quicken." With all that in mind look at John 14:16 and Hebrew 4:12 (KJV).

The word quick used in Hebrews 4:12 King James version means alive. Sisters, through the gift of the Holy Spirit we have all we need to live lives obedient to God, we're in training which takes practice, patience, and purifying. Remember, nothing will happen overnight, but trust in the power of the Spirit within you as you let the fire(s) of life's challenges bring forth the fruit of the spirit of God.

As I begin opening up about some of the times in my life when I had to be obedient, or shall I say when I chose to because let's not forget we all have been given free will. I can tell you that anytime I follow God's leading all works out for my good. As a snake sheds its skin I too have shed and removed from my life things that would keep me from allowing the light of the Lord Jesus to light the path ahead of me. It may have taken a 25-year prison sentence to realize the lifestyle of using and selling drugs, gangs, and the hustle of it all would pale in comparison to the liberating feeling as well as the truth that my life has never felt richer. I've touched countless lives while being changed by/in the process of being transformed, restored, and renewed. The power of God.

Since December 1999 I've made every choice with clarity. I love myself, my children, and my family with 100% great intention, love, and respect. I'm a mother, grandmother, student, scholar, teacher, mentor, and friend who is respected, loved, honored as well as appreciated. These are just some of the things I've been blessed to have on my resume as a child of God. Thank you, Jesus, for pulling me out of the fire and placing my feet on solid ground so that I would feast on the fruit of Who You Are.

As I'm writing, I can recall many times when my obedience was critical in order to bring forth the character that's pleasing to God, not self, and while most times my flesh was fighting to stay in control - which might I add is nothing more than pride in a box (self) with a pretty little bow on it. However, if you can trust God through the process, I promise you'll look back to a field of gold nuggets of blessings.

Growth, maturity both spiritually as well as humanly, morally balanced, strength and integrity, loving, peaceful, and every other good quality one desires when one moves from darkness to light. This is a part of being obedient unto God. I ask, "Is your fruit ripe? Or are you in the fire?" Living in the 21st century it seems as if drinking wine has become all the rage, now if one is familiar with the process that goes into setting the table with a feast and fine wine you know the process of the crushing. Similarly, like that of a brilliantly crafted Diamond, there's a process, even the way Iron has to be heated to a certain temperature in order to become pliable we have to go through a process to bring forth what God sees as our best self.

I dare say, we all have been through the crushing, or the fiery furnace of life, and through it all God knows. As Job suffered just about everything humanly possible yet as he stated in NKJV Job 23:10, "But He knows the way I take; when He has tested me, I shall come forth as pure gold." Whatever the test, whatever the trial, my sisters and brothers take comfort in the knowledge that our all-knowing, all-powerful loving God is purifying your character so that you come for as pure gold.

Restoration is an act of restoring consciousness, or health becoming revitalized as well as salubrious. Submitting to the Holy Spirit through obedience brings about A renewed spirit as well as life which in turn produces the good fruit of love, joy, peace, long suffering, kindness, goodness, faithfulness, gentleness, and self-control. As children of God, these are the qualities one should strive to gain. As I look back over my life at the many mistakes I've made as well as one horrible choice after the other, there are many things I'd love to see restored unto me or to those who have caused harm to me. However, there is no going back, and no turning back the hands of time. Nevertheless, there is a promise our mind would be renewed in the spirit. Ephesians 4:21-24 (NKJV).

God is not looking to dust us off, mend, or stitch us up, not even hide what's been damaged or destroyed. No, God is in the business of making all things new. Purifying us through the process of the fire. All the gritty dirty pieces of our lives that we try to keep tucked away God will take all of it, turn around, and use that. He will get the glory while replacing the grit, grime, and dirt with his glorious fruit. That's the key and the gateway leading us to walk in who He has called us to be sharing our tests, trials, and tribulations as a testimony all through obedience.

As I'm sitting here looking out the window from a prison cell it amazes even me to think about all I've shared in the past chapters. I say that because there are women, I've done over 20 years in prison with but due to me being a very private person most of these intimate details of my life, nobody knows. However, whether the Lord calls you to openly testify or write a book, share your life while completely vulnerable to judgment. As I did and as I encourage all to do even if your knees are knocking in the process answer the call whether it's forgiving someone you deem unforgivable follow the spirit of God, He will always lead you to peace and truth.

The truth is we are nothing without Him, but with Him, our lives will be blessed beyond measure. Is your fruit ripe for the picking? or are you still in the fire? don't get me wrong we are a work in progress so at any time the Heat in the furnace of life can be intensified or cold that depends on us individually. However, we should be continuously surrendering to God while he burns out of us any and everything that is not like him.

When I was a little girl, my father would often tell me," I'm not fussing at you, I'm telling you for your own good." Something that brings a smile to my face even at the age of 50. My point is, no matter what he told me, where he led me or asked me to do through obedience, I knew with 100% certainty that he loved me and only wanted the very best for me. Similarly, our heavenly Father also wants what's best for us, and when we decide to do things our way usually, we find ourselves in a world of trouble (hence the 25-year prison sentence I've just about completed).

In hindsight, which is always 20/20, had I been obedient to my earthly Mother and Father I would have gone to college, and continued playing sports while figuring out my career and life goals. Moreover, I'm almost certain I wouldn't have had three children by the age of 26 not to raise any of them through their most needed years. Yes, my oldest 2 were five and six when I went to prison, but oh how much of their lives I missed; all the important milestones like school graduations, first dance, first kiss, etc. It may sound silly but that's the joy of being a parent loving your children through the joy as well as pains in life.

As you know I lost my baby my youngest child at the age of 19 to Street violence, a vicious cycle, and the new pandemic that claims more and more lives each year. Now the cold-hearted reality slashed me in the face every day I'll have one less child when my family, friends, and loved ones welcome me upon my release. I often beat myself up wondering if my son was a part of my punishment. However, I know in life two things are certain, and that's life and death. More important, there's nothing we can do about the will of God, plus I wouldn't be who I am today had I not traveled along this road that the all-knowing Creator had laid out for me. I'm grateful today that I've come to understand it's in my best interest to allow God to control the steering while I trust.

Looking back over life I'm sure we can all pinpoint a time when listening/obedience wasn't our best quality. My Father would say, "Okay... a hard head makes a soft ??!!?" And I found that to be very true. Although I know my life didn't go in the direction my mother or father would have liked it to go, I'm sure they both would be proud of the woman I've become. Yes, I've taken some very bad turns ending up in more than a few ditches, I've also seen some really dark places. However, as the word of God promises in Psalms 91:14-16 (NKJV), "He will be with us in trouble and deliver us.) My Deliverance may not have come, nor look like I wanted it to, but all praise be to God, His light has landed me in an upright position while his power has protected me.

I encourage you to put your trust in the Lord and love him because he first loved you. Trust Him no matter what things may appear to be while knowing with full assurance that no matter where you're planted if you allow the living spirit of God to use you through obedience, you'll find life and joy overflowing. I'm not saying life will be a bed of roses. No, not at all, but what I am saying is the peace of God will rest on your shoulders like a fine shawl. I can testify that physical freedom doesn't always equate to "physical" freedom. It may sound cliche but it's true, some folks have been locked up so long mentally that they have not enjoyed one single day of their physical freedom.

In contrast, incarceration has allowed me the opportunity to regain true freedom again. Freedom to love myself, to make sound decisions, to be physically healthy, and most importantly the freedom to believe in myself. It has opened doors and broken-down barriers while I crossed over the margins that had once kept me outside of reaching my fullest potential. In fact, I've yet to tap into my fullest potential, and I'm freer now than I've ever been.

Yes, I've endured more than my fair share of heartache, losses, and disappointments. The deck has been stacked more than a couple of times against me...but God. My good days still far outweigh my bad days, so even when I do complain I won't complain. You are probably saying, "You lost your youngest child at the peak of Covid, your grandmother as well as your mother, and any chance of an early release, yet you're writing about obedience, faith, and holding on?" Yes, because God's grace has been sufficient today, yesterday, in 2012, 2016 as well as in 2020 when my son took his last breath.

Today I long for lungs filled with the fresh air of freedom, but I'll settle for rivers of living water flowing from my belly. oh, don't get me wrong, having Jesus is better than anything in this world, so the word "settle" has absolutely no weight to it. He is the very best one could have. Assignments through obedience come in many forms it could be through isolation that God needs to get your attention, or perhaps it's a certain person who you can't stand. However, God sees fit to use that individual to stretch me that I'm fit for the race. Whatever the assignment, trust God through the process. The word of God tells us in Romans 5:3-5 (AMP) that we are to be joyful in our trials, tests, and sufferings because through/in them our character is being proven.

After any test whether in a classroom or a practice test in life or you have a blow-up with a friend, coworker, or parent; perhaps you are led to forgive someone you know did you wrong. Whatever the case, I know when the dust settles usually both parties leave feeling better, stronger, and more mature for taking control of the situation rather than allowing it to get out of control. When being led by the spirit who is love in its fullness, is being obedient to God. Not always easy but doable.

April 2022 is one of many assignments. It had been since 2019 since I'd last seen my family and I can't count how many times the pandemic (COVID-19) had taken the world in a bag shaking it up then dropped it out upside down. I'm sure there's no need to explain the year 2020. Well, 2 years later I found myself in segregation, 24 hours after my first overnight visit since Covid. Talk about back to reality, and really quick. I went from eating fresh salad, chicken alfredo, ice cream, and snacks galore to cold oatmeal on a "seg" tray overnight. My brother tested false-positive for COVID before he departed which landed me in the seg for 30 days.

Can you say assignment? Thanks be to God I'm always trying to look at things through my spiritual eyes knowing there's always a purpose as well as a reason in every test or trial we go through.

Remember this is/was an assignment. Thirty days of isolation, and five COVID tests (all negative), yet I'm housed between two other brown girls with absolutely no clue how God strategically placed me there while shielding me to be a light to those around me. I was back in the ring fighting to stay on my feet after yet another blow to the body. However, what the enemy failed to realize is, I stay fully armored. Ephesians 6:10-18 (AMP) tells us to "be strong in the Lord and the power of His might. Pray at all times in every occasion in the Holy Spirit." I knew at the sound of that heavy steel door shutting, once I stepped into the small concrete room, this would call for some heavy prayer.

Seventeen days, two tanks, two different rooms surrounded by more than 50 people who were positive for COVID-19, and I did what God led me to do; encourage my neighbors, and help those in need as He moved me from one unit to the next When it was all said and done, yes my heart was heavy, my knees hurt and I had cried a few tears but overall, I was blessed. Opportunity to intercede for others, witness to a neighbor about who Jesus is, lift the spirits of all those women through playing gospel music and so much more. It was an assignment.

To all the women who were in the ring with me in April/May 2022, I give thanks to God for you all. Never forget prayer not only changes our circumstances it changes our hearts through the indwelling spirit of God. I returned to my regular living unit humbled, and more grateful, reminded that we are all overcomers as we share in our trials, Revelations 12:10-11 (NKJV). Continue to testify and may our every hope become a testimony.

Sisters as well as my brothers, I challenge you to elevate, raise up, and hold higher worship and praise to God for assignments are pervasive. Keep your spiritual eyes and ears open for every opportunity to be used by the great I AM, and in so doing, your life will speak the love of Christ. God has used me, my story, and my life experiences throughout the last 20+ years in ways I could have never imagined. The word of God tells me in Ephesians 3:20 (AMP) that by the power of the living God that is within me, He will do exceedingly abundantly above anything I could ever ask, think, or dream. I've seen the fruits of my labor through and by the power of the Holy Spirit. He's allowed me to be a living testimony, teacher, and preacher, as well as an example to those around me even when I didn't realize I was being watched or studied.

Through my losses, and I don't mean my loved ones only I'm speaking in terms of particular things I've worked my butt off for, yet they were taken from me by way of the ugly truth. A million brown girls deal with daily hell every second really. Racism as well as the prejudices that plague our society lays here as a foundation that this prison operates on. Everything that's available to all, well that may be so in some cases, but you better be ready to jump twice as high and speak twice as loud to get it. Oh, just not in an aggressive tone which is not aggressive at all it's assertive, yet the white fragility/privilege that's been woven into the very fabric of this country makes it so difficult to reach for, obtain, or even dare dream to be included in the "all" whether it's striving for a higher education, a second chance at life after getting off track or merely expecting the same opportunities as your counterparts

My whole point is even when you find yourself on the losing end, knees worn out from constant prayer, take a moment to reflect on how God has used you while at the same time getting the glory from your life. Hopefully, your answer is countless times, and in many ways cause that's the life of a believer. It's not easy living in this brown skin, some days the joy of it brings laughter, sisterhood, love, unity, and feelings of pride and some days the struggle and pain run deep. However, I want to encourage you my Sistah's share your pain as well as your stories because in doing so there comes healing that also brings transformation. This transformation is not only important for you but also for those lives whom you have come in contact with.

My beautiful brown Sistahs, from the deepest color of ebony to the lightest hue of cream, we are connected by the inevitable path we must travel that will determine our state of mind. Backbones of Steel so stand erect and strive to move forward in the face of whatever you've been handed, or what you've walked through thus far. I guarantee you the struggle was to enable you to breathe black magic upon another soul in order that they could carry on. When I say black magic, I'm not referring to trickery of any sort. no, I'm referring to the confusion that is set in the mind of the oppressor and the bewilderment that weighs on their faces because they have no clue how the brown girl do what she do.

It's true, you are the most resilient of all people. There's something in our blood that screams 400 years of tears. Still, we shine like black diamonds, move like silk in the wind, teeth like ivory that accentuates our skin; beautiful brown girl, remember your strength. Remember your God sitting high on a hill, and when you find your vessel empty, know that it's He that fills.

Some of my words come from a place of struggle, pain, loss even loneliness then at times you may hear from my poetic side. No matter what, or how I deliver this message of hope, and faith along with the love of Christ, it is my most humble prayer that you receive them with an open heart knowing that as God is my witness I'm writing from a place of love. *Psalms 121:1-2, Matthew 7:37-38,*

ASSIGNMENT, OBEDIENCE, FAITH

Over the last 20+ years, I can't count how many times I've been praised for my strength as well as my faith in God. it's very difficult to be handed every disappointment, every loss, every death in front of an audience of about a thousand people at best while you stand center stage given absolutely no privacy to grieve naturally nor process what life has thrown your way. I've heard it time and time again, "Lesleigh you're a strong black woman." Those words from my Sistah girls, and again the same words Echo non-stop.

I didn't know when I sat in a county jail cell in 1999 that my life, at 26 years young, would be used as a model of what God's grace in full measure looks like while walking through it all with dignity, I'd never believe it… but God (II Corinthians 12:8-12, AMP). As I share this particular portion of my life and story it's not that I boast in my infirmities, but I do testify that the strength of God has failed me not.

As we know life brings tests and trials, so it again is a job to stand through the fire for Christ's sake, after all He bore the cross for you and I. 23 years later, I echo the same words when asked how do/did I do it? "It's only by God's grace I've made it this far." Looking back on it all with 24 months left until my release, all I can say is thank you, Jesus! Acceptance and obedience go hand in hand once we as Believers can get in that space while allowing God to be our peace, our strength, and joy we can weather any storm.

Let me be clear, we serve a loving God who makes available to us here on Earth everything we need physically as well as spiritually. The word of God tells us it's our job to help one another (Galatians 6:1-2 AMP) and go the distance with our brothers and sisters in the faith. Over the years the Lord has blessed me with a loving family as well as friends who have supported me and helped me tremendously. To my God-fearing Auntie Gloria King, my uncle R.H. King, to my wonderful friend and so much more Mary Manning, who wears countless hats we've lost track of; God bless their souls for being obedient as well as faithful to the call. I'm blessed to be a recipient as they served and taught me in the process.

As I sit looking out my window, the rain pouring, I reflect as to how I got here, this woman I've become I know there's no way it could have happened without two very bright beacons of light guiding me along the way. They have held my hand, caught many tears, and heard my frustrations through it all yet tirelessly month after month year and decade after decade never complaining but always praying while encouraging me along the way - their obedience has been remarkable.

To express my gratitude in words is impossible. So, my life's mission will be to make all those proud who have been by my side. Moreover, let me not go on without acknowledging the men who have been here since day one. To my uncle R.H. and my oldest brother Alonzo King, as you both have quietly yet lovingly with complete consistency supported me, I love you. Alonzo, you made me a commitment, and you never wavered, and I say through my misfortune God turned your life around. However, that's not my story to tell, I just say we could agree you weren't living your best life. praise be to God for your obedience.

The highest forms of obedience yet due to our preoccupied lives the time we spend sitting quietly in the presence of God becomes less and less; Well things like TV, gossip, phones, etc., draw Us in more and more. Being a good listener is the key to effective communication, and I'm guilty as charged. I know I talk too much when conversing with family and friends, all I can say in my defense is I'm working on it.

Listening takes practice as well as obedience, so why do we as Believers think we aren't hearing more from our loving heavenly father? WE AREN'T LISTENING! In all our reading, studying, and praying for ourselves as well as others we're missing the point family, the word tells us in Psalms 46:10 (NKJV) to "be still, and know that I am God" ... how can we listen if we can't be still? I challenge you to discipline yourself through obedience to get into a quiet place and ask God to speak, it will draw you closer to him while enveloping you in peace and comfort. Whether you're led to pray for another, encourage, or help - whatever it is, know that God is speaking, are you listening?

FEAR

"For God has not given us a spirit of fear, but of power, love and of a sound mind. " 2 Timothy 1:7 NKJV

"When you go out to battle against your enemies, and see horses and chariots and people more numerous than you, do not be afraid of them; for the Lord your God is with you, who brought you up from the land of Egypt. 2 So it shall be, when you are on the verge of battle, that the priest shall approach and speak to the people. 3 And he shall say to them, 'Hear, O Israel: Today you are on the verge of battle with your enemies. Do not let your heart faint, do not be afraid, and do not tremble or be terrified because of them; 4 for the Lord your God is He who goes with you, to fight for you against your enemies, to save you." Deuteronomy 20:1-4

Song: "God is Able"
Artist: Smokie Norful

Song: My Weapon
Artist: Natalie Grant

Fear can paralyze one to the point that you are no longer living, but merely existing, and believe it or not, I found myself in that position a few times in my life. Fear is nothing more than a phantom if you think about it, something imagined, unreal, or made up. Moreover, it's not reality. Believe me, I'm not making light of the effects that fear can have on one's mental and emotional state. What I am saying is when a person intentionally makes the decision to separate what's real from what's being imagined a breakthrough takes place.

God is real, God is love, God is peace, and when we truly surrender our Phantoms over unto the all-powerful sufficient God who reigns victorious; we'll find the things we most fear(ed) more than likely never even happened. On this cold snowy November day, I'm brought back to a time when fear held me in its grip, it was when I learned the news my beloved mother had had a stroke. I didn't have all the information, I didn't know whether she survived it or not, but what I came to realize later was God and His Infinite love would allow me all the time needed to say my goodbye. Don't misunderstand me, because in my selfishness I wanted nothing more than my mother to make a full recovery. However, while letting go of the fear, I prayed not my will, but your will be done. (Matthew 26:42 NKJV).

My mother and I shared a love for butterflies, she would often tell me, "This butterfly has been floating around my balcony all afternoon, I knew you would call." I share this very intimate detail so you can understand the importance/ weight when I say I knew the exact moment she transitioned. It felt like a butterfly had burst from its cocoon, captured inside my heart. it was then I knew this was God's will, and I didn't have to fear anymore.

Whether you find yourself standing in the Gap through intercessory prayer asking God to help, heal, or protect fear is usually there in the mix. As I said in my previous chapter loss is a difficult thing to deal with, whether it's slowly saying goodbye to a friend who has lost the battle to cancer, or a loved one who has been down in the straight jacket of mental illness as Believers we have to call on the power and peace of God, (2 Timothy 1:7 AMP).

In 1999-2000 as the months went by, and the reality set in that I not only was facing 25 years in prison, it also became painfully obvious I would not be leaving KCJ to go home. As weeks turned into months, and months into a year - when all was said and done, I spent almost two years awaiting my fate; oddly enough not in fear. I wasn't afraid, and in hindsight, I didn't believe it was going to happen, and now that I'm 24 months from my release I am testifying that as God was with the three Hebrew boys in the fire, he has walked with me. see the Book of Daniel chapter 3:21-25.

Let's fast forward 20 years. It's March 2020, the beginning of what would turn out to be a global pandemic which produced a fear in people worldwide like no other. The last recorded pandemic of this magnitude was 100 years ago, so to say we weren't prepared is an understatement. However, for me as well as every other believer, I knew our trust was in the lord, the only one to be feared. 2 Timothy 1:7 tells us God didn't give us a spirit of fear but of <u>power, love,</u> and a <u>sound</u> mind. Even as a blood-bought child of God in this flesh, it's very challenging to move as a faith-filled Believer as folks are dropping like flies. Moreover, our history proves that incarcerated people as well as African Americans have been used as test dummies in which vaccines are administered. [see footnotes]

Worldwide, most people were forced to wear masks, isolate at home, and were cut off from family and friends, as well as accepting they could no longer work. As I'm writing this book a few months literally from it being a full 3 years, there's

still a sense of fear in the atmosphere. in short...
this was a fearful time.

In prison, we are all part of the same fabric, just as
Believers are members of one body in Christ.
However, having no control over HVAC systems
or food prep (just to name a couple of things),
imagine how a brown girl(s) would feel when out
of the blue CDC comes with a vaccine. Fear of
losing your own life, or the lives of loved ones
caused most people to get vaccinated, but some
didn't. I prayed taking my concerns to my daddy,
and even in my hesitation, I took the first initial
vaccine. Trusting God for the outcome with zero
boosters, I'm here to give God the glory I've never
got covid. Sadly, my brother as well as his whole
family, nine in total, wasn't as fortunate, and my
sister ended up hospitalized fighting for her life.
praise God with lots of prayer God had mercy on
her, she pulled through.

Prayer has been and will always be my go-to. God
is first in everything! Proverbs 3:5 and 6 tell us to
"Trust in the Lord with all your heart leaning not
on your own understanding... he shall direct your
path." Sistahs and brothers God is good, loving,
and full of grace, so it wouldn't do you justice if I
didn't lead you to verses 3-4 of the same passage. I
encourage you to trust in the favor of God, and

while losing my son at the peak of COVID I rested in the all-sufficient hands of my Lord rather than allow fear to consume me. Whatever you're facing, whether one of life's storms or a situation that appears hopeless, remember prayer is our weapon, and nothing is looming too large that should cause us to shrink in fear.

What became painfully clear to me several months into this pandemic, as well as throughout, was whether one suffered from mental health issues, or didn't realize they were walking a tightrope, I had been called to intercede heavily for those close to me. Whether someone you're in a relationship with, your child, or a stranger, it's hard falling asleep at night not knowing if your loved one will give in and take their own life. After all, we are fighting a spiritual warfare, and I had been faced with both. However, I did my job. I prayed, fasted, and poured rivers of Living Water whenever I got the opportunity.

[Harvard Civil Rights CLLR. (Shackled by Science: The Exploitative use of prisoners in scientific experiments"] Nov. 14, 2018

My Hope and prayer is that even while my son is still missing today in my transparency you will be drawn to your knees, interceding for all those known and unbeknownst to you that the peace of God would keep them in heart as well as mind. Let no fear overtake you when fighting for every thread within the fabric that is us the body of Christ!

I've covered some very tough subjects that have pushed me way outside my comfort zone, but if I haven't learned anything over the years, I've learned you're not growing unless you're uncomfortable. With that being said, it's time to talk about the act of forgiveness. Something we find difficult to do yet we expect it from God without fail. Take a deep breath, sit up, and get ready for the Holy Spirit to open some wounds. Some wounds may be old, or new, whatever the case - have no fear. God is able.

FORGIVENESS

"And forgive us our debts,
As we forgive our debtors." Matthew 6:12 NKJV

"Bearing with one another, and forgiving one another, if anyone
has a complaint against another; even as Christ forgave you, so
you also must do." Colossians 3:13

"Then Peter came to Him and said, "Lord, how often shall my
brother sin against me, and I forgive him? Up to seven times?" 22
Jesus said to him, "I do not say to you, up to seven times, but up
to seventy times seven." Matthew 18:21-22

Song: Deliverance is Available
Artist: Vicki Yohe

Song: You Know My Name
Artist: Tasha Cobbs Leonard

There are many things in life that have proven to be difficult, yet we continue especially when the end goal is worth more than the struggle we had to endure. As we get into this very arduous topic of forgiveness, it is my prayer for the freedom I found through forgiving rather than holding on to old wounds, anger, and resentment you would also find freedom.

Formula: Open the heart valve... let go!

I can't tell you exactly how to get there, how long it will take you, or at what point you'll have an epiphany that will leave your eyes wide open to the truth, the act of forgiveness lifts you to a higher place. We have all been offended, and we have all offended someone else, so no matter how deep the pain, or how ugly the scar is when you reach that high place as a victor, not a victim it's pure bliss.

Believe me, I'm very well aware that it is of the opinion some things are Unforgivable. However, if God chose to charge us with every sin, fault, or crime we've committed where would we be? After all forgiveness isn't at all saying it's okay, it's pardoning while making room for God to do what we can't. the Bible says the Lord will judge, Hebrews 10:30-31 NKJV and vengeance is His.

As we move forward, and while I share arguably some of the most intimate details of my life, I ask that you open your heart valve letting go of all the gunk and grime. it's between you and God - let go.

Song: Anthony Brown ft. Naomi Raine - 1st Exchange (Live)

On February 19th, 2022, as my daughter and I were talking on the phone about my release which never fails to come up, she shocked me saying, "Mom, I want you, me, and my aunties to sit down together and conversate." This came as a shock to me, because over the years of my incarceration relationships have been broken as well as hearts. My response was I believe we can do that. However, it has to begin with open-hearted forgiveness.

Over the last couple of decades, I've had to learn as well as put into "Praxis" the art of releasing people, along with myself, to find true forgiveness. True forgiveness is the most liberating feeling one could possibly experience after years of bondage, more importantly, and especially when the bondage is self-inflicted. No matter what has held you captive, no matter what demons you struggle with due to past trauma, or traumas in your life, there's nothing like taking back your life as well as the power to live free through forgiveness.

Self-forgiveness is oftentimes more important, or shall I say needed, in order to truly offer with sincerity forgiveness to another. However, when the two meet it's a beautiful union. Seeing as nobody's exempt, and we've all caused pain or offended another at some point in our lives as well as been on the receiving end, it's our job to either ask or offer a pardon. As women and men of God we do ourselves, or others, no good by holding on to grudges, counting wrongs, etc.., and at the end of the day until we can walk with a clear conscience, holding no charge against our brother or sister, friend or spouse there's work to be done.

The Bible tells us in the book of Ephesians 4:26 "Be angry, and do not sin, do not let the sun go down on your wrath." Clearly, God gave us emotions and feelings for a reason, so it's not a sin to feel those emotions. However, it is a sin to allow them to fester which leads to resentment as well as unforgiveness. I find myself asking forgiveness daily while repenting for sins known and unbeknownst to me, it's a constant battle yet in every way worth all the growth I've made. Now getting back to my sister(s), specifically my oldest sister whom I love deeply, and always looked up to. Alohnna exemplified strength, and dedication to family as well as demonstrated early in my life what an academic scholar looked like. All these qualities and more I'd be able to look back on as I began building myself up from the bottom when I started my 25-year prison sentence.

Moreover, I realize that whether one vanishes from your life, or not when you're down in every sense it's up to you how you'll respond. I learned over many years we were all sentenced. Yes family, friends, and loved ones, but everyone did the time the way they knew how. Moving in love, and making space in my heart to constantly pardon those connected to me has become a lifestyle that comes with being a woman of God, and how can I not be in my imperfect blemished self?

As I'm looking out at this midnight blue sky it reminds me of many dark days, I spent clawing my way back to the surface of where real life was taking place. I reminded myself there was no Darkness nor death that Jesus couldn't pull me out of. 1 Peter 2:9 tells me that I am a chosen people, a royal priesthood and God has called me out of the darkness. So, it is important to remind yourself, encourage yourself, and build yourself up on your most Holy faith. We are Daughters of a King.

At 26 years old and never having had a felony before, to say I was ignorant to the laws then as well as now is an understatement. However, sadly it would be years into my incarceration that I would learn what the "accomplice liability" law meant. I say all this to bring attention to how I as well as "a million brown girls" sit where I sit even today 23 years in. Either it's "legalized blackmail" where you're forced to accept a plea offer for something you didn't do or go to trial to be hanged, it's a sick so-called Justice System that's never been set up to serve people who look like us.

Bottom line, I wasn't the shooter and wasn't at the scene of the crime, yet I got more time than anyone! was there a lot to forgive surrounding how I came to be incarcerated? Yes. However, I too had to beseech forgiveness from my co-defendant and late son's father. As I said nobody's exempt. Over the first five years, it took me a lot of soul-searching, and heart-scraping work to begin what I know now as the breaking down to build back up process. I attended every self-help group, and non-violent Communications Workshop, I roll-swapped, prayed, and completely stripped myself down to find true forgiveness in my heart regarding my victims. I'm sure as you're reading this book you may ask, "How is it that I had to find it in my heart to forgive the victims?" Well, I speak the truth, and there was much to forgive. However, I say that with every bit of compassion for the family.

I'd like to be clear, I've made very callous decisions in my past, even in this particular case, and by no means do I claim to be without fault. What I am saying is I'M NO murderer, nor have I ever been. If I can convey anything that would be of value to you that is…forgiveness is key to freedom! Twenty-three years in on a 25-year bid, cast into a system that was meant to break me, but what they failed to realize was you can't break what you didn't make to begin with. God is a promise keeper, and for every problem, there's a promise. The Bible tells us in Isaiah 61:3 "To console those who mourn in Zion, to give them beauty for ashes…that He may be glorified." In life we will mourn, we will at times carry a spirit of heaviness, but God will plant us as trees of righteousness beside still waters.

When I was a young girl, I was sexually abused, and molested, between the tender ages of 8-11 years old by a family member who should have been protecting me. However, it's always the ones closest to you that do irreparable damage. At this point in my life, I feel no need to name names, but what I do feel is important to note is how very empowering it was the day I confronted my abuser. Naming what was done to me, no longer covering the ugly truth, after almost 20 years of silence, afraid to speak out of fear it was over.

On 12/12/99 I had to speak out because now I had two children to protect, and looking at going to prison I couldn't risk my own daughter's innocence to be stolen the same way mine had been stolen. Have you ever had a deep cut that began to heal due to covering it, or allowing it to dry? Now can you recall how painful it was to have the scab pulled off by accident? All you could do was scream, well the only way a cut will heal is to uncover it. Uncovering the wound, or pulling off the scab leaving "secrets," with no room to hide, but fully exposed starts the healing process. Healing is critical in order for one to live free.

I remember the day, I remember voicing the words, "You owe me an apology." I remember silence, I could feel his shame, guilt, and embarrassment yet I didn't care! It was about me not him. It was about me finally freeing myself of the unmerited guilt, shame, and dirtiness I felt with every memory, every dream that invaded my sleep which calls me to relive over and over and over his sickness laid upon me.

Through lots of therapy, yes therapy, I was able to work through the trauma, not all of it but I am in a good place. God in my life has allowed me to love this person, and to forgive totally and completely while moving forward. I'm not saying I haven't had times when I slip, I have. However, I live free without the "cover". I'm free to write my story in power while giving an open window into my life by way of many experiences.

I want you to see forgiveness is possible, and I'm just a regular brown girl from the hood. I'll leave you with this, let love in, it will cast out all fear and will dispel all (hidden scars) darkness tries to cover. Moreover, the Bible tells us in order for our Heavenly Father to forgive us, we too should forgive, Matthew 6:14-15.

On March 27th, 2022, I found myself sitting in my room pondering a question posed in my prayer Journal. "What are some everyday things I'd like to talk to God about in prayer?" Automatically it brought me to the day I was informed that my son had been murdered alongside his cousin, yes, a double homicide. The question still lingers, who did it? Would they ever be held responsible? do they know Christ as lord? will I ever meet them?

I know all these questions may not seem normal, but for me, I believe in the transforming power of God. I believe in forgiveness, and restorative justice as well as praying for the lost souls of our youth. Very early on after learning of what happened all I could do was pray for whoever had committed this crime and ask why. One would naturally deduce that my initial response would be anger, hate, or disdain towards the perpetrator(s). However, the Holy Spirit led me to do all I knew to do. On one hand, it wasn't my natural choice or decision, and God only knows it wouldn't bring either him or his cousin back. Prayer was the solution and the only answer I heard as I continued to ask why.

Having experienced the most devastating, soul-crushing blow ever when I lost my mother, losing my son leveled me. I knew that if I wasn't very careful, I would find myself at the mouth of the same black, dark hole of depression that met me when my mother died. I couldn't go back to that place, not ever. Let me be very clear, so as not to be confused I most definitely felt anger, hurt, confusion, and a deep dislike for whoever had done this. Moreover, not having a clue who could leave two young men riddled with bullets vanish without a trace...unfathomable.

Losing a child leaves a parent wrestling with feelings/ emotions you weren't even aware you had, and hate, unforgiveness as well as anger were at the top of my list. I'm human, I'm fallible, and as a good friend of mine often says, "Girl I'm half baked" undone and more importantly a work in progress. There's no way to measure one's grief, or any particular response you should expect, just know that God's grace is sufficient. God's grace will pitch a tent over and dwell upon you. 2

Corinthians 12:9 (AMP), His strength will be made perfect in our weaknesses through any danger, or troubles in life, but remember we have a job. Our job is to lead our lives as living testimonies, as ambassadors of Christ, as lovingly with compassion and powered by the Spirit as possible.

People of color know all too well by way of experience as well as witnessing the very unbalanced, disproportionate sentencing regarding people of color. It covers us like the darkness of the night sky, hence the reason the U.S. has more people incarcerated than anywhere else in the world. Their answer is "Lock 'em up and throw away the key." My answer to Justice being served against the person, or persons, who murdered my child wouldn't be to lock them up for life, or 60+ years which = life. No that would only make me a part of the already existing problem. However, I would be more interested in looking them in their eyes while I empty my heart into their soul. Moreover, meeting them with compassion, and making the statement true forgiveness is more difficult than throwing away a life.

After serving 23 years as a mother, as a woman of God, and unfortunately a convict/throwaway in the eyes of society, I'm here to tell you that I'm in search of a real solution to what appears to be an epidemic within our urban communities. It's time we begin reaching our youth, hand in hand, and heart-to-heart asking the question, "What led you to this?" Then listen and respond.

If I had had someone listen to me, pour into me, and believe in me as well as my visions as a kid into my young adulthood I can almost guarantee you I wouldn't be telling this story from prison. In order to see the trajectory changed it is time we change our approach. Yes, a life for a life just not in the sense Society deems justifiable, because for most people of color especially African Americans that equals 20-60 years in prison. Please let me be clear, I don't condone nor excuse crime, murder, etc. I believe that you do the time if you do the crime. However, it's painfully obvious that for black/brown faces, justice looks as different as black from white.

This is my story, my heart, and all I'm saying is I believe in true transformation of mind along with educating/empowering. In fact, if we could outfit our youth with the proper tools, they'd be an asset not a liability to their community. As God dealt with me in the midst of me processing my son's death, I knew in/while he did His work, I knew He would use my experience for something far greater. It was my job to stay connected to the true vine because through Him healing my heart He was also helping those around me.

The facts are that as I have lived my life here in prison for the last two + decades, unbeknownst to me, God had been touching lives through my own in the process. As I said, all I've done with intention each day has been to live out John 15:1-5 as I've gone through my valley experiences, my many losses as well as my high points. Remember all hasn't been doom and gloom. I've accomplished much while sharing my joy with tons of beautiful women over the years.

Before I bring this chapter to a close, I want to remind you that usually while a person is going through a trial your only focus is getting through it, and not on the onlookers as well as how you're being studied. However, whatever healing or restoring one's life looks like, again, remember it's not always about you. God is faithful even when answered prayers don't show up the way we'd hope for, but Psalms 37:4-5 (Amp) states if we delight ourselves... He will give us the desires of our hearts. If it's healing, He'll do it. Forgiveness, He'll give it. Hope, He is all hope. Love, He is the epitome of love, so much so He gave his own son.

John 3:16 something no human I know is willing to do.

For me, in December of '99 I lost more than freedom, and since then even more. However, I haven't lost my hope in the living God who has kept me all these years. I encourage you my brown girls to hold on to the unchanging hand of God, if family has abandoned you, friends have disappeared, lovers have left Jesus says behold I stand at the door... with me. Revelation 3:20 (Amp). Open the door to your heart, and experience what having a friend in Jesus feels like, I guarantee you won't be disappointed.

Forgiveness is liberation, so whether you're guilty or innocent, or you fall somewhere in between, it's time... break the chains that have held you in bondage to unforgiveness for x number of days, months, or years. Begin by lifting the heaviness of anger, guilt, shame, pain, and any other negative feelings that have attached themselves to you which in turn will allow you to begin the healing process while living free. God bless you; God's peace be upon you; God shine His light and love on you.

RESTORATION

21 Fear not, O land;
Be glad and rejoice,
For the Lord has done [a]marvelous things!
22 Do not be afraid, you beasts of the field;
For the open pastures are springing up,
And the tree bears its fruit;
The fig tree and the vine yield their strength.
23 Be glad then, you children of Zion,
And rejoice in the Lord your God;
For He has given you the [b]former rain faithfully,
And He will cause the rain to come down for you—
The former rain,
And the latter rain in the first month.
24 The threshing floors shall be full of wheat,
And the vats shall overflow with new wine and oil.
25 "So I will restore to you the years that the swarming locust has
eaten,
The crawling locust,
The consuming locust,
And the chewing locust,
My great army which I sent among you.
26 You shall eat in plenty and be satisfied,
And praise the name of the Lord your God,
Who has dealt wondrously with you;
And My people shall never be put to shame." Joel 2:21-26
(NKJV)

*Song: **Run Til I Finish***
*Artist: **Smokie Norful***

The word restore according to the Merriam-Webster's Dictionary is defined as 1: to give back: Return 2: to put back into use or service 3: to put or bring back into a former or original state.

Early on in my sentence, God gave me the scripture/promise in Joel 2:21-26, and although at the time I had no clue as to how absolutely true and faithful God would prove to be in his word. However, as I sit here 23 years later, I can honestly say that I am a living testimony to God's restorative power. Even today as I look back over the years recalling the many trials, losses, heartbreaks as well as every growing pain I know the woman I am today is due to the indwelling spirit of God. I don't by any means claim to be whole or complete in myself, and I know I've yet to experience all that God has for me in the form of my latter rain.

Locusts come in many forms in our lives here on earth, and whether they have shown as swarming, consuming, or chewing destruction is just what it means to ruin. I fell victim to the plots, plans, and schemes of the enemy which has left me in ruins, but thanks be to God for His amazing grace. I don't know what in your life is representative of being eaten up by the various locusts, but what I do know is there is no level of destruction that God can't rebuild. The Bible tells us we are complete in Christ in Colossians 2:10, so no matter how long we believe the lies of the enemy, Jesus awaits our return to Him the living truth.

Is it the loss of your children? Is it years of your life? Perhaps it's been your health, or youthfulness due to drugs. Well, you're NOT alone. Whatever it is believe me God is a restorer of ALL things. While conversing with my peers, or just talking to random people about life's experiences, our past etc. Most of the time I get the same response. It's so hard for folks to believe I once lived the life I once lived; gangs, drugs, violence - you name it I most likely did it. However, it shows how God can take a mess like me and use me as a message.

My attitude was ugly, my heart was full of stones (see Ezekiel 37:25-29), but God... through the washing of the word I was slowly brought back to my original state. The destructive things/people in my life that tried to snuff out the light of the Spirit failed, and I began to seek God above all else...the rain fell.

Finally, my Sistahs, ask the Holy Spirit to show anything, anybody, and everything that the Locust has eaten up in your life. Now by faith as a born-again believer in Christ Jesus, ask Him to begin the restoration process. Now step by step allow God to prove Himself faithful. As you begin to regain your life, and your light, share your story/testimony of the goodness of God.

Song: I'll Trust You Lord
Artist: Donnie McClurkin

Being incarcerated does have its benefits, but that's something decided in the mind of each individual as they walk out of their prison sentence. One can decide to wash oneself of the unhealthy habits, and way of thinking along with anything else that led you down that path of destructive behavior. There's an invigorating feeling one gets after a long, good night's rest, or a nice hot shower after a long day at work. You feel fresh and energized. You feel restored. Getting to a place where you can think clearly, make healthy choices, and set healthy boundaries while looking forward to the finished product is exciting.

I'm fully aware that everyone's life journey is unique and different from the next person's. So, whereas it takes time for some, it may take little for others. However, when the opportunity presents itself for a reboot, restart, or refresh grab a hold and don't let go. Be open and willing to be sheared like a sheep, letting everything/everyone fall off that fails to bring positive energy to your life.

Love yourself, be good to yourself, respect yourself, and above all honor yourself every step of the way. It's important that we work towards being the best version of ourselves which means daily making a conscious decision to envision yourself in the best health possible. With 100% intention of making it your business to apprehend emotional, spiritual, physical, mental, and psychological balance in order to live a purposeful, healthy life. This is what the process of restoration has looked like to me.

The last two decades were spent working, and if I could compare the work to something it would be to that of making a quilt, fitting each square that has been cut very precisely as well as measuring top to bottom, side to side to ensure the quilt would fit together ending with a warmth providing cover. When I think of warmth in terms of the renewal process, I'm talking about one's heart being changed, the stones being removed while God replaces them with gems like compassion, love, and grace towards all women/men. The fleshly heart only God can restore (return) from wherever we lost it.

Let's not forget that any good quality quilt has to be fitted with a quality batting, or feeling which gives you weight. The weight in the renewal process is protection, or God's glory. There's something about the glory of God about His weight, and power nothing can stand up against the great El-Shaddai (Almighty God) Genesis 17:1. Learn to trust, you can always call on the "batting" in any battle as long as you're rooted and grounded and immovable in the faith. (I Cor. 15:57-58). Depending on one's particular style, and aesthetically speaking, who wouldn't want a quilt that is pleasing to the eye? The look, or appeal comes into play when onlookers can see the transformation through the restoration.

I've heard it so many times as well as confessed it, "Thank God I don't look like what I've been through." God has a way of bringing back your glow as He washes the dirt of your past hurt(s), any addictions that held you captive, whatever it is if you'll trust God, you'll begin to see yourself aesthetically beautiful again in a new light. Now wait... with things having been returned unto you, your heart has been changed, you're walking in the protection under the weight of God, and you got your glow! Now it's time to reap the benefits.

You'll notice folks will look at you differently, they'll speak to you in a different tone with respect, and honor as you've been honoring yourself by putting in the work. You'll begin to see the impact that your life is having on the lives around you and it will begin to mean something to you. Moreover, you'll become more and more honored to be a vessel used by God.

It's a wonderful feeling when you're walking in your newness with not even the slightest bit of resistance, now I'm not saying it's easy, or I'm perfect I slip up daily. In fact, what I am saying is my strength comes from God, and the Bible tells me that God's strength is made perfect in my weakness (2 Corinthians 12:9) therefore when I fail, I call on Him for help. I want to break down the word as well as the meaning of re-newal, re-store, re-do, re-match so you can get in your Spirit what's available to you. "Re" is to start over, so anytime you see "Re" as a prefix to a word, that's giving you the permission to accept the fact that you're worthy of a new start.

New is to be made new, a clean slate, and just as Christ was resurrected from the dead in order to give us an opportunity at a new life, and life eternal with Him once this life here on earth is over. He also offers us a renewed life in Him here on Earth. Here comes the rain of a renewed, restored life in Christ Jesus, are you ready to be drenched in the

Living Spirit of God? Look up, the downpour is falling. Do you dare stand underneath the rain of God's blessings? My sistahs, it's time for restoration.

Song: Dear God
Artist: Smokie Norful

Song: Greater is Coming
Artist: Jekalyn Carr

Song: 1st Exchange (Live) [featuring Naomi Raine]
Artist: Anthony Brown/Naomi Raine

Song: Alabaster Box
Artist: CeCe Winans

12/17/22

LIFE UPDATE

Lesleigh: On August 25, 2023, I became the very first woman in the state of Washington, as well as the Country (from my understanding), who has walked out of Prison in plain clothes, no handcuffs, and no shackles as a regular civilian while still fulfilling my sentence.

I was escorted by my Superintendent, a Lieutenant, a unit Supervisor, and the assistant to the superintendent, who took all the photos. I was asked back in April 2023 to write a proposal of what re-entry would look like to me, seeing as my sentence disqualifies me for work release, G.R.E., or any other program that would allow me to slowly assimilate to being a moving part of society.

Long story short, roughly 4 months later, through the AMENDS, I was taken on my first outing to a public trail where we walked roughly 2 miles, picking blackberries. I was also taken to eat lunch at a nearby McDonald's where we sat for 45 minutes. I ordered my own food while dining amongst other folks who had *no clue* that I was an inmate. Oh, that's not all. We then went to a local Crumble Cookie for dessert. Mind you, this is the first time in almost 24 years I've been out in public, I was even able to pet a woman's dog on the trail.

This is the first of many to come as I wrote up a 3-phase re-entry plan that includes doing more things like this in phase 1, e.g., going to stores, parks, etc. Phase 2 will involve setting up a bank account for myself, doing job readiness things, and learning the latest technology, and phase 3 possibly having family visits. As you know, my release date is 12/11/2024, so not only am I excited to be allowed to open the door for other women in my same position, but I'm blessed that God chose me for this opportunity. There will be an article written up with lots of photos as three organizations were working together to make this happen: Norway, California, and Washington.

A true testament of His faithfulness. I couldn't have ever imagined or written this in my story. Ever.

Other Books Published by Authors Inside

Authors Inside is a 501(c)(3) nonprofit organization empowering incarcerated and formerly incarcerated authors to make sustainable change through narrative writing, with the purpose of reducing and preventing juvenile crime, promoting and maintaining safe communities, and improving the welfare of youth and families.

Made in United States
Troutdale, OR
07/22/2024

21383351R00066